The New Social Story Book

Illustrated Edition

Revisions by Ms. Carol Gray

The stories in this book were originally written
for children and adults with autistic spectrum disorders by students
in Mrs. Sandy Johnson's psychology and sociology classes
at Jenison High School in Jenison, Michigan.

Edited by:

Stacy Arnold
Damon Burg
Carol Gray
Kelly Goward
Sarah Hayes
Luke Jenison
Carie Jonker
Sue Jonker
Karen Lind
Joe Smiegel
Steve Wesorik
Chad Zuber

Illustrations and Cover Design by Sue Lynn Pauken

All marketing and publishing rights
guaranteed to and reserved by

FUTURE HORIZONS INC.

Future Horizons, Inc.
721 W. Abram ● Arlington, TX 76013

800-489-0727 ● 817-277-0727
817-277-2270 fax

Website: www.FutureHorizons-Autism.com

E-mail: Edfuture@onramp.net

ISBN 1-885477-66-X

This book is dedicated to:

Mrs. Viola Schuldt

in recognition of her many contributions

to children and adults with autistic spectrum disorders.

"The more I learn, the more I can do."

—Tyler Steketee
Social Story #57

Preface

Children and adults with autistic spectrum disorders (ASD) struggle to read, interpret, and respond effectively to their social world. From their perspective, the statements and actions of others may at times seem to occur without meaning or identifiable purpose, occurring randomly and without warning or logic. To those working on their behalf, the same experience may be echoed; parents and educators may report that a child is demonstrating a behavior that seems to occur "for no apparent reason" or totally "out of context". Social Stories address this social confusion by requiring parents and professionals to first stop and consider a situation from the perspective of the child or adult with ASD, and second to identify and share information that may be missing with a Social Story. The result is often an improvement in social understanding on both sides of the social equation.

This book was first developed in 1994, and revised and updated in 2000. It contains Social Stories written by psychology and sociology students at Jenison High School, in Jenison, Michigan. The students were trained to write Social Stories by Carol Gray, the consultant to students with autistic spectrum disorders for Jenison Public Schools. The popularity of the book spread with the increasing number of presentations and workshops on the topic of Social Stories. Experience with Social Stories rapidly expanded, resulting in an improved understanding of the approach and modifications in the original guidelines that define each Social Story. Efforts to revise the text to comply with the newly revised guidelines, and to illustrate the stories, began early in the year 2000. The result is an illustrated and updated version of a book that has already proven its success and popularity.

In their own way, all books reflect the people and knowledge of the time they were created. A few books take on a timeless quality, addressing issues that find a place in each progressing year. Similarly, it was the hope of the psychology and sociology students that the stories they wrote in 1994 would hold value for children and adults with ASD for many years to come. Adolescence is that time in life where many events and activities take on a timeless quality –holding the importance of a milestone. A book like this, containing the work of authors on the verge of high school graduation, by its very nature reflects their idealism, and their hope that they have contributed something of importance to the lives of people with ASD that might endure the test of time.

This editor has not forgotten their enthusiasm, and felt a responsibility to reinvest in their efforts by updating their words to give their stories a "fresh coat of paint". The addition of simple, clear illustrations brings additional meaning to the text. Just as important is one aspect of this book that is *unaltered*. The topics for all of the stories are as relevant and important today as they were in 1994. Perhaps this is due to the fact that, while we add detail to our understanding of people with autistic spectrum disorders, many of the events and skills that are the most challenging for them remain the same. For that reason, all of the stories from the first edition of this book are also in this second edition – with new wording and the benefit of improved insight. On behalf of the authors of the first edition, best wishes for social success.

Acknowledgements

This book was made possible by the investment of time and creativity by the following individuals:

Sandy Johnson —A psychology and sociology teacher at Jenison High School, Sandy has worked with the special education staff, for several years, to expand programming for students with autistic spectrum disorders. Her cooperation, enthusiasm, and investment of time were invaluable in the development of this book.

Psychology and Sociology Students —Over 250 students contributed stories for possible inclusion in this book, Unfortunately, several factors limited the number of stories that could be printed. The stories were terrific, and the students were hopeful their stories would be a part of the book. Sincere appreciation is expressed to the students at Jenison High School, 1993-94, for the quality and sincerity they brought to their assignment.

The Editing Committee —Several students volunteered to assist in editing and typing the 100 stories in the Social Stories Book 1994. Their talent and determination literally made the final manuscript for this book possible. A very special thanks to the following members of the Editing Committee: Stacy Arnold, Damon Burg, Carol Gray, Kelly Goward, Sarah Hayes, Luke Jenison, Carie Jonker, Sue Jonker, Karen Lind, Joe Smiegel, Steve Wesorik, and Chad Zuber.

Jenison Public Schools —Sincere appreciation is extended to the administration and staff of Jenison Public Schools. Their acceptance, concern and support has created an environment where projects like this book can be successfully undertaken and completed. Specifically, thanks to: Vicki Bliss and Tim Staal, who patiently shared their expertise with computers; Martha Sweedyk, for her advice and assistance; and the administration of Jenison Public Schools for their support of efforts to share information with parents and professionals from the United States and abroad.

How to Use this Book

This book is organized into thirteen chapters. Each chapter contains several stories. A quick review of the Table of Contents provides a general idea of how this book is organized.

Page numbers are not listed in the Table of Contents, and pages are not labeled sequentially throughout the book. To locate a story, refer to the story number listed to the left of the story title in the Table of Contents. This number appears in large print in the upper right hand corner of the first page of the story. To locate the story in the book, refer to the numbers in the upper right hand corner at the beginning of each story. Stories are numbered sequentially throughout the book.

Page numbers are listed sequentially *within* each story. These numbers are listed in the center of the bottom of the page. The story number is listed first, followed by the number of the page within the story. For example, the first page of story #87 is indicated as 87-1. The only exception to this are stories which contain only one page, in which case numbers are not listed at the bottom of the page. A page number at the bottom of the page indicates there is more than one page to the story.

Most stories will serve as an outline. They can be used to create a final story that fits the needs of an individual student or situation. With many of the stories, adding possible variations of a given situation may be helpful. In addition, aspects of a story that do not apply can be eliminated. Some stories focus on the same topic, and may be combined and edited to draw on ideas from different authors.

Stories may be presented to a student using any one of a number of formats. The story may be placed in protective clear plastic sheets in a narrow three-ring binder (business supply stores have 1" three-ring binders, some with plastic insert covers, which are perfect for this). Stories may also be cut apart. The spacing between concepts in each story make this easy to do.

The final chapter, "How to Write a Social Story," provides information on developing stories *from scratch*, and how to implement them. Those wishing to write a Social Story will find information in this chapter.

"When it is time to eat spaghetti,

I put my fork in the spaghetti and slowly twirl it around.

I am careful to only put a mouthful of spaghetti on my fork,

So it will fit in my mouth."

—Erin Klooster
Social Story #34

Table of Contents

Chapter 3: Personal Care Cont.

Chapter 4: Cooking and Mealtime Routines

Chapter 5: Helping Around the House

Chapter 6: Outdoor Games/Activities

Chapter 7: Time for School

Chapter 8: Getting Around

Chapter 9: Community Helpers

Chapter 10: Restaurants and Shopping

Chapter 11: Understanding the Weather

Chapter 12: Holidays, Vacations and Recreation

Chapter 13: How to Write a Social Story

Chapter 1
Social Skills

Learning to Chew Gum

Sometimes people chew gum.

Usually they chew one piece at a time.

Sometimes gum comes in a wrapper to keep it clean. It's important to take the gum out of the wrapper before putting it in my mouth.

It's a good idea to try to chew my gum with my mouth closed. That way I will chew my gum quietly.

I will try to leave my gum in my mouth while I am chewing it.

When my gum has no more flavor, I may take it out of my mouth and put it in the waste basket. Sometimes, before I put my gum in the waste basket I might put it in a tiny piece of paper or tissue.

Giving a Gift

A gift is something you give to someone.

People give gifts to other people .

Some gifts are big.

Some gifts are small.

When I give someone a gift I might say,

"Here's a gift for you."

Sometimes people give me a gift.

When people give me a gift, I will try to say, "Thank you."

Saying "thank you" is polite.

People like to hear "thank you" after they give someone a gift.

Happiness is a *Good* Feeling

Sometimes people smile when they are happy. Smiling makes people feel good. When I smile, people know I am happy.

Things that I *like* often make me feel happy.

Some things that I like are_____,

_____, and

_____.

Learning to Help Others

Sometimes people need help.

Sometimes people need help opening a door.
Sometimes people need help making dinner.
Sometimes people need help in other ways.

People like to be helped.

It's helpful of him to hold the door open.

Her hands are busy pushing the stroller. I'll help by holding the door.

Thank you.

Let me hold the door for you!

Sometimes people do not need or want help.

If I see someone who I think needs to be helped, I may ask that person, "Do you need help?"

The answer may be, "No." This is okay.

The answer may be, "Yes." I may ask, "What would you like me to do?"

If I think I cannot do what they ask me to do, I may try saying, "Can you show me what to do?"

How to Give a Hug

I can try to learn to give a hug.

I spread my arms apart.

I wrap my arms around someone.

I gently squeeze that person.

That is how to give a hug.

How to Greet Someone

There are many ways to greet someone.

When I see someone I know, usually I will try to smile and say "hello."   They may say "hello" back. They may stop to talk with me.

Sometimes I will try to shake their hand. Sometimes, when I am visiting a relative or a close friend, I will try to give them a small hug or a little pat on the back or the shoulder.

There's someone I know!

Hello.

Sometimes, if I am just passing someone I know, I can smile, wave, or just nod my head. Most people like it when I smile at them. Smiling can make people feel good.

How to Make Someone Happy

Many people like to see smiling faces. I can make someone happy by smiling at them.

Many people like being hugged. I can try to make people I know happy by hugging them.

When I say "hi" to someone, it makes them happy.

People like to feel happy.

How to Use the Telephone

Many people like to talk on the telephone.

Sometimes my grandpa or grandma will call me. We talk on the telephone.

Sometimes other people call me on the telephone.

When people call, I will try to pick up the telephone receiver and say, "Hello."

The person who is calling will return my greeting.

Sometimes I will not know the person calling on the telephone. Then it's a good idea to ask who is calling.

Sometimes people call and have the wrong house. This means they have called the wrong number. I can tell them, "I am sorry. You have called the wrong number." Then I can say "goodbye" and hang up the phone.

Sometimes I may want to call someone. To do that, I can learn to pick up the telephone receiver and dial their phone number.

When someone answers the phone I can try to say, "Hello."

I can talk to my friend on the phone.

Learning to Play Fair

It is a good idea to play fair with my friends.

Sometimes my friend may win the game we are playing.

I will try to stay calm if my friend wins a game.

If my friend wins a game, I may ask them to play again. Asking to play again is a friendly thing to do.

It is good to play fair when playing games. That way friends may want to play again.

Receiving a Treat in School

Sometimes someone will give me a treat at school.

It might be something to eat for a special occasion. We may have treats to share the fun of a classmate's birthday. We may have treats to celebrate a holiday.

The person who brought the treat has to make sure that there are enough treats for everyone.

When someone gives me a treat, I will try to remember to say, "Thank you."

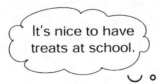

Sharing

I may try to share with people. Sometimes they will share with me.

Usually, sharing is a good idea.

Sometimes if I share with someone, they may be my friend.

Sharing with others makes them feel welcome.

Sharing with others may make me feel good.

Sharing Toys

Many children play with toys. When they play with toys, they have fun.

It may be fun to play with toys with other children.

I can learn to share toys.

Sharing might be fun. When I play, I will try to share and have fun.

I'll have a turn again. We throw the ball back and forth.

Smiling

People like others who smile.

Smiling shows others that I am happy.

I will try to smile when I am happy.

Sometimes if I do not smile, people may think I am sad or angry.

I may receive compliments if I smile.

13-1

Smiling often makes others feel good.

Learning to Shake Someone's Hand

When I meet new people, they sometimes hold out their hand. People do this as a way to say "hello."

I can put my right hand toward theirs and tightly squeeze their hand. I will try to look at the person and smile. Sometimes they will smile back. After holding hands for a short time, each person may let go.

I can learn to feel comfortable with this new way to say "hello."

When do I say, "Thank you"?

Sometimes people do nice things for me. When someone does something that makes me feel good, I will try to say, "Thank you."

Sometimes people help me. When someone helps me, I will try to say, "Thank you."

Sometimes people share with me. When someone shares something with me, I will try to say, "Thank you."

Thank you.

15-1

Saying "thank you" may make me feel good. Saying "thank you" also makes other people feel good.

Saying "thank you" is a nice thing. Other people will know I am a nice person.

When do I say, "Excuse Me"?

Sometimes people may be in my way. When there is a person or group of people in my way, it is a good idea to say, "Excuse me."

I will try to be very nice to the person or group of people when I say, "Please excuse me."   Usually, people will move out of my way.

I like it when people are nice to me. I will try to be nice to them.

Excuse me.

17

Looking While Listening

When someone is talking to me, I try to listen. This is a very nice thing to do.

Looking at the person who is talking to me is helpful. This lets the person know I am listening.

Sometimes I try to look at a part of their face. I try to do this so the other person knows that I am listening to them. The person who is talking to me will like this a lot.

Chapter 2
People and Pets

Can I hold the baby?

Many people like babies. Babies need to be handled gently.

If I would like to hold a baby, it's important to ask permission from an adult.

The baby will feel safe if I sit quietly while holding the baby.

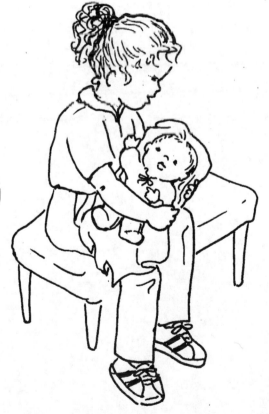

When I am done holding the baby, the adult will carefully take the baby.

I can move when the adult has the baby in their arms.

Sometimes I will thank the adult for letting me hold the baby.

I Have a Cat

I have a cat. Many people like cats.

Usually my cat likes to be petted. Cats feel soft.

Cats purr when they are happy. When I pet my cat, it may make me happy, too.

It may be fun to pet my cat.

Playing with My Dog

I have a dog. My dog is furry and likes to play. My dog's name is

_____.

Sometimes I play with my dog. I throw a ball and my dog runs and brings it back.

When my dog is tired of playing, I might sit down and pet my dog. Dogs have soft fur. Many dogs like to be petted. They wag their tails when they are happy.

My dog can be one of my best friends.

Chapter 3
Personal Care

21

Nightmares

Sometimes I may have a nightmare when I am sleeping. Nightmares are the same as a dream, but more scary.

Events in nightmares do not really happen. They are like pictures in my mind.

It is all right if I am scared. I may try telling myself it is all in my mind. It is only a dream. Adults can help children with nightmares, too. It is okay to ask an adult for help with nightmares.

When I wake up, I will see that I am all right.

Using the Shower

Learning to use the shower may be fun. My mom or dad may help me with my shower.

The first thing I do is go into the bathroom and close the door. This keeps my shower private.

Next, I take off my clothes. This keeps my clothes dry.

After that, I turn the water on and make the water temperature comfortable. A comfortable water temperature is important for a comfortable shower.

Next, I make sure the water is coming from the shower head. It comes out as a spray, like rain.

Most people stand when they take a shower. I try to stand up in the shower.

I get in the shower and get wet. This helps me get clean.

After that, I wash my hair. I take a little shampoo out of the container and rub it through my hair. This makes bubbles that clean my hair.

It's important to rinse all the shampoo away. I will try to run water through my hair to get all of the shampoo out of my hair.

Clean hair is nice to see and touch.

Next, it's important to wash my body. I will try to wash my body by using the soap and rubbing the soap all over my body.

Then I will try to rinse my body off in the water. It is important.

I like to clean my body. It makes me smell nice.

Usually when I am done, I will try to turn off the water. Then I'll step out of the shower. This keeps the floor dry and safe.

After I step out, I usually dry myself by rubbing the towel all over my body. This makes me dry.

I dry off so my clothes will not stick to me. This helps to keep me comfortable.

After drying off, I will try to put my clean clothes on. Then I am done.

My Shower

People like it when I smell good.

Many people think showers can be fun and refreshing.

Sometimes the water sounds like a slow, calm waterfall.

It's okay to get in and let the water fall on me.

I may like the warm water and the smell of soap on my skin.

After I clean myself with soap and use shampoo on my hair, I rinse all the soap and shampoo off.

I dry myself usually with a towel.

The shower makes me clean.

Most people take a shower every day.

Learning How to Shave

Some people need to shave. Adults shave. Men often shave.

Some people do not need to shave. Little children do not shave.

Shave cream makes shaving easier and safer.

When men shave, they only need to put shave cream on the part of their face that needs to be shaved.

Men carefully shave their faces.

It's important to be very careful with razors. They are sharp.

When men are done shaving, they will wash their razors and put them away.

Washing My Hands

Sometimes, my hands get dirty. It's healthy to wash my hands when they are dirty.

This is a list of steps people follow when they wash their hands:

1. Go to the sink.

2. Turn the water on.

3. Get hands wet.

4. Put soap on hands.

5. Rub hands together.

6. Rinse hands under the water.

7. Turn off the water.

8. Dry hands on a towel.

These steps will help me learn to wash my hands. It may take a little time to learn how to wash my hands. This is okay.

Why do people wash their hands?

Sometimes hands get dirty.

Most people wash their hands when they are dirty.

Sometimes hands need to be washed at other times. This is okay. For example, sometimes I cover my mouth when I cough. My hands may get germs on them when I sneeze. Sometimes hands may get germs on them when I use the toilet.

It's a good idea to wash hands when they have germs on them. It's also a good idea to wash hands before eating.

My parents are happy when I wash my hands to stay healthy.

Why do people wear clothes?

People wear clothes.

People have different clothes for different seasons. When it is cold, clothes keep people warm. In the summer, clothes protect people from sunburn. That way, the clothes people wear help them to stay safe and comfortable.

In the winter, I may wear coats, gloves, scarves and boots, because it is very cold.

In the summer, I may wear t-shirts, shorts, and sandals. These are clothes that help to keep me cool.

Sometimes it rains. It helps keep me dry if I wear my rain coat and use an umbrella.

Sometimes I go swimming. It's intelligent to wear a swimsuit. Swimsuits are made to get wet.

Clothes help people in a lot of ways. Clothes help me.

Wearing My Shoes

I usually wear my shoes when I go outside.

Wearing shoes helps keep my feet clean and safe.

Sometimes I put one pair of socks on my feet before putting on my shoes.

Then I put a shoe on each foot.

It can be fun wearing shoes.

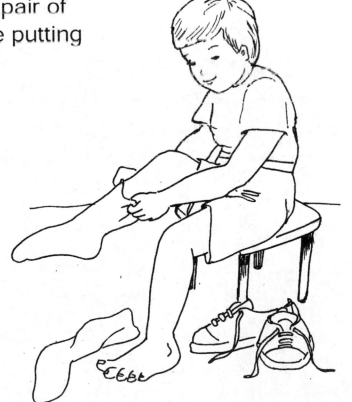

My New Shirt

Sometimes I need to buy another shirt.

I might need a t-shirt, a sweat shirt, or a button-down shirt.

Sometimes I go with my mom or dad to the store to buy a shirt.

I look for shirts that are the colors I like. Sometimes I may need a shirt of a certain color.

When I find a shirt I like, I might have to try it on. Then I can see if it is the right size.

Sometimes when the shirt is the right size and color, I can give it to my mom or dad so that they can buy the shirt for me.

30

Keeping Others Healthy When I Cough

Sometimes I am sick.

Sometimes being sick makes me cough.

When I cough, tiny germs come out of my mouth. Germs can make other people sick, too. People do not want to be sick.

It's important to cover my mouth with my hand each time I cough. I will try to cover my mouth when I cough.

Thermometers

Sometimes I use thermometers. When I am sick, my mother needs to check my temperature.

There are many kinds of thermometers. Adults know how to use a thermometer to take my temperature.

The adult looks at the thermometer so that they can tell how hot I am inside.

Usually if I am too hot inside, I am sick.

Chapter 4
Cooking and
Mealtime Routines

How to Make Brownies

Usually before I make brownies, I ask my mom or dad if it is ok.

The first thing I do when I make brownies is wash my hands.

I need a brownie mix, oil, eggs, and water to make brownies.

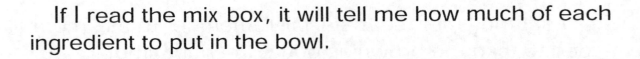

I need a big bowl in which to mix the brownies ingredients.

If I read the mix box, it will tell me how much of each ingredient to put in the bowl.

When I make brownies, I will try not to spill. If I spill, I can get my mom or dad to help me clean up the mess.

Once the ingredients are stirred, I have to put the brownie batter in a greased pan.

Next, the brownie batter goes in the oven. My mom or dad can help me put it into the oven.

I will always try to be careful when I am around the oven, so I stay safe.

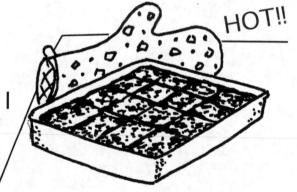

HOT!!

The brownie mix directions list the right time and temperature to bake the brownies. Sometimes the brownies go in the oven for about 25 minutes at about 350 degrees.

I set the timer, so that I will remember to ask mom or dad to take the brownies out at the right time.

When the brownies are done, Mom or Dad usually takes them out of the oven with a cooking mitt. They wear a cooking mitt so they won't burn their hands.

It's important to turn off the oven.

I have to let the brownies cool for about 15 minutes. I put my dirty dishes in the sink, so I can wash them.

After the brownies are cooled, sometimes I may eat one.

Sometimes I like to eat brownies and drink milk.

Eating at the Table

Usually, people eat meals at a table.

This makes it easier to eat neatly and safely.

I will try to sit at the table while I am eating.

Mom likes it when I eat at the table.

How do I eat spaghetti?

Sometimes my mom or dad makes spaghetti for dinner.

Some people like to put tomato sauce on spaghetti. Some people like spaghetti plain. People eat spaghetti in different ways.

When it is time to eat spaghetti, I will try to put my fork in the spaghetti and slowly twirl it around.

I will try to be careful to only put a mouthful of spaghetti on my fork. That way it will fit in my mouth.

34-1

Some people use a napkin to wipe their mouth when they eat spaghetti.

Many people like to eat spaghetti.

Great Manners for the Dinner Table

Dinner is usually the last meal of the day. It is often the largest one, too.

I usually eat dinner with my family. We usually eat at the dining table. We eat at the table because it is easier to eat and talk.

When I eat dinner, I will try to only eat from my own plate. If I want more food, I may ask for it.

Most people are careful when they eat. I will try to keep food on my plate or in my mouth.

How do I set the table for a meal?

Children can learn to set a table. I am learning to set a table. Here are the steps:

1. If there are things on the table, I need to take them off and put them in a better place, so they will not get dirty.

2. When I set the table for a meal, I usually need to get plates, cups, forks, knives, spoons, and sometimes napkins for all the people who will be eating with me.

36-1

3. I need to set a plate, a cup, a fork, a knife, a spoon, and a napkin at each place where someone will be sitting.

4. At each place where someone will sit, I place the fork on the left side of the plate, and I place the napkin, knife, spoon, and cup on the right side of the plate.

My mom or dad will be very happy with me for setting the table.

Why is it important to chew quietly?

I am learning to eat so others stay comfortable.

Many people like others to chew quietly.

It is polite when people close their mouths when they chew.

Many people learn to chew with their mouths closed. This is a part of learning good manners.

At mealtime, I will try to take small bites and try to chew with my mouth closed.

Learning to Say a Prayer at Mealtime

Sometimes my family says a prayer before we eat our meal.

Prayers are a time when the whole family or one member shares their worries, thoughts, or thanks.

Prayers are usually a quiet time to praise God.

I will try to be quiet and keep my eyes closed when prayer is taking place.

People usually open their hands and eyes when the prayer is finished. My mom or dad will tell me when we are done.

39

Some People Try New Foods

When I am eating, I may see food that I have not tried before. I will not know what it tastes like unless I try some.

Sometimes people ask me to try a new food. That's because they think I may like it.

I may like to try new foods. Sometimes if I like it, I can have more.

If I do not like it, it's okay to say, "No, thank you."

Trying new food is a good way to discover which foods I like to eat.

40

Learning to Eat Healthy Foods

The five major food groups are meat, dairy, bread and cereal, vegetables, and fruit.

It is important for people to eat food from the five major food groups.

Eating foods from the five major food groups helps me stay healthy.

I will try to eat healthy food.

It makes others happy to know I eat healthy foods to keep my body growing strong.

Chapter 5

Helping Around the House

When to Clean My Room

Sometimes my room gets messy. Many clothes and toys may need to be put away.

When my room gets messy, I may need to clean it. Sometimes my mom or dad will ask me to clean it.

I will try to pick up my toys and put them away.

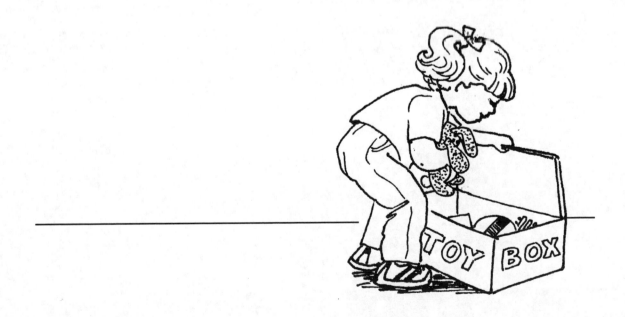

I will try to pick up my clothes and put them away neatly where they belong.

Mom and Dad like to see my room clean.

42

Making My Bed

After I wake up in the morning I get out of bed. Making my bed will help my room look neat. I may want to learn to make my bed.

I will try to straighten the sheets on my bed.

I will try to straighten the blankets on my bed.

I will try to place the pillows up at the top of my bed.

Then my bed is made. My parents will feel happy to see my bed made. They will feel happy to see I have learned something new!

43

Learning When to Turn Off Lights

I will try to remember to turn the lights off at the right times.

Sometimes when I am in a room, I may need to have the lights on. Especially at night, I can see better with the lights on. Other people may need lights on to see, too.

If no one needs a light on, it may be helpful to turn it off.

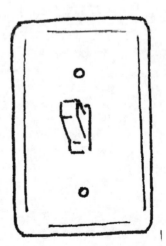

If I turn the lights off, my family saves money.

Mom and Dad can help me learn the good times to turn off lights. Mom and Dad will be happy with me if I turn off the lights at the right times.

Turning Off the Lights

The lights allow me to see when it is dark.

The lights help me to see what I am doing.

The lights help others see what they are doing, too.

I may turn the lights off when no one else is using them.

Vacuum Cleaners Clean Homes

My family has a vacuum cleaner .

A vacuum cleaner cleans rugs and carpets. Vacuum cleaners turn on and off.

Some people like the sound of the vacuum cleaner. Some people like it better when the vacuum is turned off.

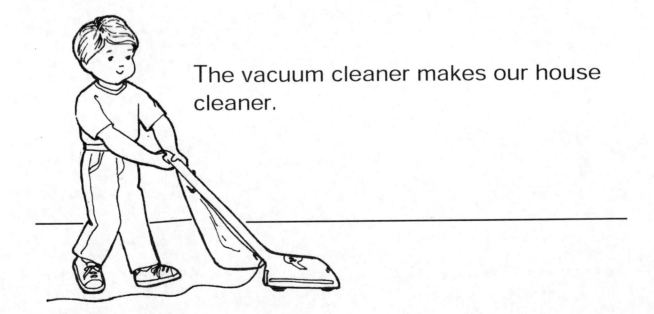

The vacuum cleaner makes our house cleaner.

When do I get the mail?

Sometimes I get the mail.

I know the mail is here if I see the mail person put the mail in the mailbox.

Usually I do not see the mail person put mail in my mailbox.

Sometimes other people may get the mail from the mailbox.

Sometimes the mail person is early. Sometimes the mail person might have car trouble, or they might be a little late.

Sometimes the mail person does not bring mail. On Sunday the mail does not come. Sometimes on holidays the mail does not come.

I will ask my mom and dad when I should go and get the mail.

My mom and dad can tell me when the mail is not going to come.

Chapter 6
Outdoor Games/ Activities

47

May I pick the flowers?

Flowers come in many colors, shapes, and sizes.

Some flowers smell nice. Some flowers smell okay.

Sometimes I may pick flowers if I ask an adult first. I must say, "May I pick the flowers?"

I will try to ask an adult if I may pick the flowers.

Sometimes the flowers must stay in the ground. This is okay.

Time to Play Quietly

It is fun to play.

Sometimes I run, jump, and yell when I play.

Sometimes when I am playing, others may ask me to be more quiet.

I will try to play quietly when asked.

Others may help me find a quiet play activity.

Why should I play outside?

Playing outside may be fun.

Sometimes when children play outside, they feel better.

Sometimes going outdoors makes children feel refreshed or excited.

Sometimes I may play with toys outside.

I may play outside with my friends. They may like to play outside, too.

Sometimes I may swing on the swings.

Sometimes I can hear the wind.

Playing outside may be fun.

49-2

Chapter 7
Time for School

Getting Ready in the Morning

I am learning to get ready for school.

I am learning to comb my hair and brush my teeth in the morning.

Sometimes I may take a shower in the morning. That way I smell good and look good.

After I wash myself, I will try to put on my clothes. Usually I change my clothes every day.

Sometimes my parents or guardians will tell me which clothes I should wear.

Most people like to eat breakfast in the morning. Sometimes I eat breakfast before I wash and get dressed.

Sometimes I eat breakfast after I wash and get dressed.

I will try to get up at the time my parents or guardians tell me. I will try to learn to wash myself, get dressed and eat breakfast.

Then it is usually time to go to school.

How can I walk to school safely?

My name is _____. I am in the _____grade.

I go to _____ School. I am learning to walk to school.

_____ walks with me to school.

Usually when we leave my house in the morning, we walk on the driveway to the sidewalk.

There are a lot of things to look at outside. It is very important to think about walking to school safely.

It is important to know the way to school. I need to know which way to walk.

Walking with someone helps me learn the way to school. To be safe, I need to stop when the sidewalk ends at a road. Then I need to look for cars.

If I see a car that is close to us, we need to wait until the car goes by. We will walk together across the street.

To be safe, we must remember to only talk with people we know.

I am learning to walk safely with others to school.

52

Riding the School Bus

Some children ride to school on a bus.

Usually the bus will pick me up and bring me to school.

Some children like riding the bus. They think it is fun.

Usually the bus will pick me up from school at the end of the day and bring me back home.

Sometimes I will not ride the bus. Mom or Dad will tell me when I will not ride the bus.

Having a Substitute Teacher

Sometimes my regular teacher is gone. She may be away learning new ways to teach. She may be ill. On those days I will have a substitute teacher. A substitute teacher knows how to help children learn.

My regular teacher wrote a note to my substitute teacher. She left lesson plans, too. That way the substitute teacher knows what to do.

I will try to treat my substitute teacher like I treat my regular teacher. The substitute teacher is trying, too. I will try to follow the rules of my regular teacher with the substitute teacher.

54

Listening to the Teacher

It is good to listen to the teacher. The teacher helps us learn. Listening makes it easier to learn. The teacher likes it when the children listen.

If I have a question, it's okay to raise my hand and wait for the teacher or someone who will help me.

I will try to listen when the teacher is teaching.

Sometimes we might have a substitute teacher. When this happens, I will try to listen to the substitute teacher.

What should I do when the teacher is talking?

I go to school almost every Monday, Tuesday, Wednesday, Thursday, and Friday.

There are many other children at school. In my classroom, the children usually sit at their desks.

When the teacher is talking to the class, the children are usually quiet. When someone wants to say something, they usually raise their hand and wait for the teacher to call on them.

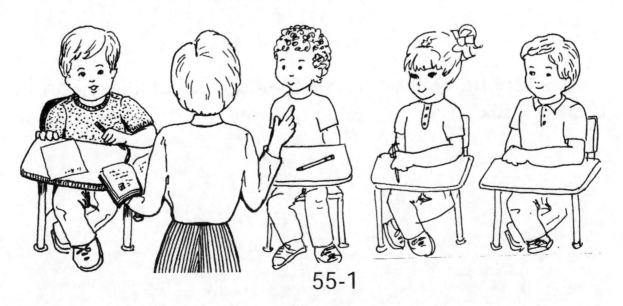

55-1

When the teacher is talking to the class, I will try to be quiet and listen.

When I want to say something or answer a question, I will try to remember to raise my hand and wait to see if the teacher calls on me.

Sometimes the teacher may ask another child to answer a question. Sometimes the teacher will give another child a chance to talk. I may be called the next time.

The teacher will be happy if I try to be quiet and listen.

The teacher will be happy if I learn to raise my hand before I talk.

Getting My Turn to Talk in Class

There are many students in a classroom who like to talk.

It is hard for a teacher to hear one student talk if everyone else is talking, too. Many times it's important for one person to talk at a time. In a classroom, people need to take turns talking.

When I want to talk to the teacher in class, I will try to raise my hand and sit quietly.

Sometimes the teacher will call on me to talk. I may have to wait for my turn to talk.

If I want to talk to the teacher during class, I will try to raise my hand and wait for the teacher to call on me.

Learning Ways to Stay Calm in Class

Sometimes school is fun. Feeling calm in class can help me learn.

If I need help to stay calm, my teacher can help me. My teacher may help me learn ways to stay comfortable.

Staying calm in class will help me understand the teacher. I will try to work with my teacher to learn to stay calm in class.

Help for Frustrated Children

Sometimes children have difficult school work.

Sometimes, when children have difficult school work, they feel frustrated.

Feeling frustrated is okay. I will try to learn to stay calm when I am frustrated.

Many children ask their teacher for help if they need it. Teachers can help children who feel frustrated.

It is okay to ask for extra help from teachers. If I need help on school work, I will try to ask for help.

Asking a Question in Class

When I am in class, sometimes I have a question.

When I want to ask a question, I try to raise my hand and wait until the teacher calls my name. If I raise my hand, the teacher will know I would like to ask a question. When the teacher calls my name, that means it is my turn to ask my question.

The teacher will try to answer my question.

I will try to listen carefully to my teacher's answer.

Other children may have questions, too. Sometimes my teacher will call another name. I will try to
wait patiently and quietly until my teacher calls on me
to ask my question.

Could you please repeat that?

When I do not understand something that is said to me, it's okay to ask that person to repeat what they said.

I can try to look at the person and say, "Could you please repeat that? I don't understand yet." This is an intelligent thing to do.

> Could you please repeat that? I don't understand yet.

The person will repeat what was said. It may help to hear it again.

What am I supposed to do at recess?

Usually, I have recess most of the days I go to school. Sometimes one recess is in the morning, and the other is in the afternoon.

Recess is a time that I may go outside. I may walk and run around. I may also talk out loud. I may do other things, too.

When I am in class, I often need to sit still, be quiet, and do my work. I try to listen to my teacher.

When I go outside, it's okay to talk and move around. I may choose what equipment I want to play on. Usually there will be things to climb, slide down, or swing on.

I may also play a game, if I want to, with some of the other students. Sometimes I may play tag or baseball. I may play by myself. Playing alone is okay.

Recess is a good time to get rid of some of my extra energy that builds up while I am sitting quietly in class.

When recess is over, I may feel ready to sit down quietly in my classroom again. It may be fun and helpful to have recess.

Assemblies

There may be times during the school year when my schedule changes. Sometimes I will go to an assembly.

Many students think most assemblies are fun.

If I have an assembly, my teacher or another adult will tell me when it is time to go and where to go.

62-1

When I have an assembly, there are a lot of people there. Usually it is not just my class.

Sometimes we go to an assembly to listen to someone speak. It's important for children to sit quietly. That way each child can hear the speaker.

I will try to listen to what the speaker says. Usually it's polite to clap when the speaker is finished speaking. I will try to clap when everyone else claps.

There are times when we go to spirit assemblies. This assembly involves the whole school. Sometimes at these assemblies it is okay to cheer and be noisy.

When I go to these assemblies, I will try to watch what other students are doing, so I know what I am supposed to do. If everyone is cheering, it is okay if I cheer.

Watching other children may help me know what to do at an assembly.

When the Fire Alarm Goes Off

Sometimes as I sit in class, I hear a buzzing alarm go off. The alarm may mean we are having a fire drill.

A fire drill gives students a chance to practice for a real fire. Usually, there is not really a fire.

My teacher waits for me to line up with my class at the door. It's important to walk quietly with my class.

63-1

I will try to walk calmly outside. It's important to wait until my teacher says that we can go back inside.

The fire drill is over when my teacher leads us back inside.

64

What do I do in a fire drill?

Sometimes at school we have fire drills. They are only practice. Usually, fire drills only last a short time.

Usually, there is not a real fire. I have to practice just in case.

When I hear the alarm, I quietly get up from my seat when my teacher tells me to.

I stand in line with my class and we walk outside with our teacher.

When the fire drill is done, I can go back to my classroom.

65

Afternoon Announcements

Each day we listen to afternoon announcements. I try to be quiet and listen.

It is important to be quiet.

I will try to sit and pay attention. What they say is important to me. I will try to listen, so that I know what is going to happen.

That is why I listen to the afternoon announcements.

Why should I do homework?

During the week, I usually go to school.

While I am at school, my teacher might assign homework for me to do. Sometimes I want to do something else instead.

If I do my homework, I will probably learn new things and maybe practice what I have already done.

When I am told to do my homework, I will try to do it the best that I can. This is an intelligent idea.

Chapter 8
Getting Around

Escalators

Escalators can be found in many stores.

I can use them for going up or down.

Escalators are very safe when used in the right way.

I must make sure I know which way the escalator is going.

After I step onto the escalator, I hang on to the railing until the moving stairs slide under the floor in front of me.

When the stairs slide under the floor, the floor is not moving.

Many people think escalators are fun to use.

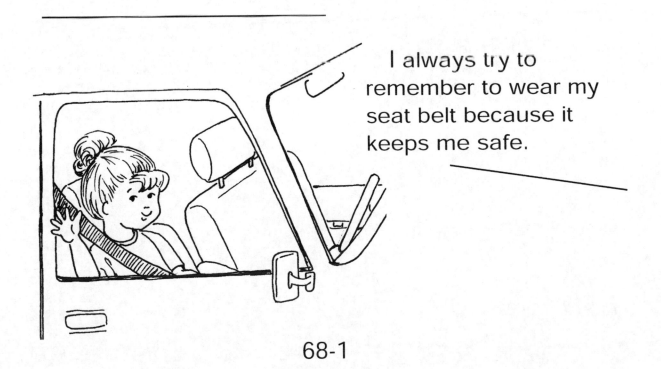

Riding in a Car

When I need to go away, I usually ride in a car.

I ride in cars with people I know, like my family. Sometimes my parents or teachers tell me it is okay to ride with them.

I open the car door when I get in the car.

I always try to remember to wear my seat belt because it keeps me safe.

It helps the driver concentrate when I try to remember to sit quietly in the car. I need to try to remember to keep my hands to myself. I need to talk quietly when someone is driving.

When I am riding in a car, the door is closed. The driver stops the car and tells me when it is okay to open the door and get out.

69

Riding in the Car

Sometimes, we ride in the car and travel to other places.

When we get in the car, we open the door of the car and sit down.

We use seat belts to stay safe. To put on my seat belt, I grab my seat belt strap, put it over my lap, and connect the two seat belt ends.

When I ride in the car, I try to sit still, watch the scenery, or play quietly.

Wearing Seat Belts

When I get into a car, it's important to fasten my seat belt. My seat belt keeps me safe.

It's intelligent to keep the seat belt snug. This helps to keep me safe.

When I get into an automobile, I will try to grab the seat belt strap, find the handle, and push it into the holder. When I hear a CLICK sound, I know my seat belt is fastened. I know I'm safe.

I am safe in my seat belt. That is why I try to always wear a seat belt.

71

Why do I have to wear a seat belt?

Usually when my mom or my dad go to the store or go away, they usually go in a car.

Sometimes I go with them. They always want me to wear my seat belt. My mom and dad ask me to wear my seat belt. They love me and they do not want me to get hurt. Sometimes a car bumps into another car. It is important for me to wear my seat belt, so I won't fall out of my seat.

I will try to always buckle up.

Chapter 9

Community Helpers

Going Through the Car Wash

Sometimes the car gets dirty. The snow or rain or other things splash up from the road. The car looks dirty.

One way my mom or dad wash the car is by taking it to the car wash.

Car washes can be interesting. Sometimes, I might get out of the car and watch the car go through the car wash. Sometimes, I stay in the car with my mom or dad. We ride through the car wash.

The car goes in the car wash. The water comes down to rinse the car off. If I stay in the car, I will stay dry because the car will protect me. I am safe.

Next, the soap comes down. The soap gets the car clean, just like the bath soap gets me clean.

Next, two or three sets of brushes scrub the car. They make a sound.

I will try to relax because I know I am safe. The brushes are outside the car and I am inside.

After the car is scrubbed, more water comes down to rinse away all the soap.

The water stops. The car moves through some long cloth-like towels hanging from the ceiling. The cloths dry off the car.

The water gets blown off the car by big hot air blowers. The blowers are noisy.

I am still safe.

The car may move through more cloths hanging from the ceiling.

The car wash is over. The car Is clean.

72-3

Going to Worship

Sometimes people
go to worship.

Some people think
going to worship is fun.
Sometimes during
worship, I am able to
sing with others. When I sing, I will be sure I can hear
the person next to me. That way I know I am singing
at the right volume.

Sometimes I will sit next to someone I do not know.
If they say "hello" to me, it is polite to say, "hello."

It is respectful to sit quietly while the pastor, priest,
rabbi, or someone up front is speaking. There may be
a lot of people. If I am asked to speak, I should speak
quietly, so I do not disturb other people.

How to Sit Still During Prayer

I sit in church on Sunday. We sit in church to hear announcements and a sermon, and to sing songs. Church usually lasts about an hour.

The minister talks to me and many other people. When it is time to pray, the minister usually will say, "Let us pray."

We bow our heads, close our eyes, and put our hands together.

When the minister is praying, I will try to be quiet and sit still. This is an intelligent thing to do.

When the minister is done praying, he says, "Amen."

Sometimes the minister does not say, "Amen." My mom and dad will let me know we are done.

After the minister is done praying, we open our eyes.

Sometimes someone other than the minister prays. I will try to act the same as when the minister is praying.

I will try to sit quietly when someone is praying.

Going to the Library

The library is a quiet place. It is quiet so each person can read or work. Many people need it to be quiet to read or work.

I can get books to read. Sometimes I can rent videos or read magazines.

The library is a place where I can study, do my homework, or look up information that I might need to know for class.

When I am at the library, I will try to be quiet. This helps others who are visiting the library.

If I have a question or need to talk to someone, I should try to *whisper* quietly.

If I find a book that I like, I can read it at the library, or I can bring it home.

If I want to bring it home, I must go to the front desk and give the clerk my books.

The clerk will check them out, so I can bring them home.

The clerk writes or stamps a date in the front cover. This is called a due date. This is the date I have to bring the book back. It's okay to bring the book back *before* the due date.

Sometimes, I need help finding a book that I want. I can go to the front desk or find a person who works at the library to help me. I can ask them to help me. Usually, they will be happy to help me find a book.

Why do I get my hair cut?

My hair is constantly growing.

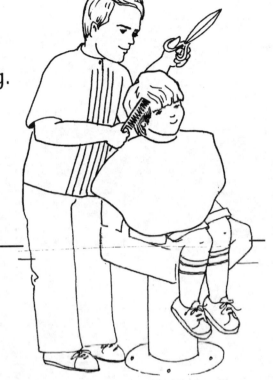

Sometimes hair needs to be cut.

Barbers are trained to cut hair. It does not hurt when the barber cuts my hair.

I will try to remember that it is safe to get my hair cut.

Chapter 10

Restaurants and Shopping

An Eating Experience

Sometimes I go out to eat at a restaurant with my family. I may have a fun time when we go out to eat.

Sometimes we go to a big restaurant. Sometimes we go to a small restaurant. Sometimes we are seated by a waitress or waiter.

When we go out to eat, it's important to listen to adults. It's important to follow restaurant rules.

Usually, there are other people eating at the restaurant.

I usually choose what I want to eat from a menu. I will try to be kind to the waitress or waiter.

Waiting for a Table

When I go to a restaurant, there might not be a table that is ready for me.

There may be other people who are also waiting for a table.

Some of those people may have gotten to the restaurant before I did, so I will have to wait for my turn.

Sometimes there is a list of people waiting for a table. As their names are called, a hostess crosses their name off the list. I can put my last name, or the last name of someone I will be eating with, on the list.

Soon our name will be called. When our name is called, it is our turn and there will be a table for us.

Going Out to Eat

Many people like to go out to eat.

When people go out to eat, they may get dressed up, depending on where they are going. Mom and Dad will tell me if I need to get dressed up.

Sometimes I may have to wait in line before I may be seated. That is okay. I will be seated soon.

When I am seated, I may look at the menu to see what I want to eat and drink. I may tell Mom and Dad what I want to eat and drink.

When the waiter or waitress comes to ask what I would like to eat, I will try to tell her what I would like.

It may take a while for the dinner to come, but we will get our dinner. Sometimes we get the drinks before the meal.

Talking in a Restaurant

Sometimes my parents or relatives like to go out to eat.

Sometimes they take me along. It can be fun to eat in a restaurant.

My parents or relatives will let me know what kind of restaurant we will go to. If it is a fancy restaurant, I may be asked to wear nice clothes. Mom or Dad can help me choose what to wear.

In a restaurant, I will try to talk quietly. Other people like to talk to the people at their table without interruptions.

When I talk softly, the other people I am sitting with can usually still hear me.

I will try my best to talk quietly.

When is it okay to eat with my fingers?

Sometimes my parents like to take me out to eat.

When we are at the restaurant, someone may show us to our table and give us menus.

My parents will help me order my food. They know what food is affordable and good to eat.

When I get my food, most of the time I will need to use my silverware.

It is okay to use my fingers to pick up food that falls in my lap. I can pick it up and set it on the edge of my plate.

Sometimes it is also okay to use my fingers. I can ask if it would be okay to use my fingers.

If it is not right to use my fingers, the silverware is the best thing for me to use.

Eating in a Restaurant

Going to a restaurant is different than eating at home. There are other people eating there, too.

I may sit at a table. The menu has lots of foods listed on it.

I will try to use my best manners when around other people.

The waitress asks me what I would like to eat. I tell her what I have chosen and she goes to get it.

Sometimes the wait is long. It's important to try to wait quietly for our food. I will try to wait patiently for my food to come.

82-1

My food will be served on restaurant plates. That is okay.

When I have finished eating, the waitress will bring a bill for the food that I ordered. Sometimes there are even little mints with the bill.

After the bill is paid, it is okay to leave the restaurant.

Going Shopping

When I go shopping with my parents, they already know what to buy. Sometimes they make a list, other times they remember what we need.

When they make a list, I may look at the list and try to find the items on the shelves.

Sometimes I want a special treat. It is okay to ask my parents for a treat if I see something I would like.

My parents know what is best for me. They will tell me if it is all right to get a treat. They may say, "No." They may say, "Maybe another time."

Getting New Shoes

I wear shoes on my feet to keep them warm and protect them.

Sometimes my shoes get old and wear out. I sometimes need new shoes.

Sometimes I go to a shoe store to get new shoes.

A man or a woman will help me find new shoes that fit my feet. My new shoes will probably be a little bigger than my old shoes.

84-1

I will try to be quiet in the shoe store. Getting new shoes may be fun.

Chapter 11

Understanding the

Weather

Hail

Hail is a part of nature.

Hail is little pieces of ice that fall like rain.

The sound of hail hitting things sounds like fast tapping.

I am safe inside.

Rainy Days

The weather isn't always nice. Sometimes it rains.

When it rains, water falls from the sky.

Sometimes it is okay to go out in the rain. I will ask an adult if it is safe to go outside.

I should wear a jacket or take an umbrella when I go out in the rain. A jacket or umbrella will help to keep my clothes dry.

How to Make A Snow Angel

When winter comes, snow may fall. The snow is wet and very cold.

Some children like to play in the snow.

Sometimes the snow tickles when it lands on my skin.

Sometimes I am able to play in the snow. I might like to make snow angels. Snow angels are pretty.

When the snow falls, I wait until morning and ask my mom or dad to help me put on my outdoor winter clothes.

First, I put on my clothes so that I will stay warm. Sometimes my winter clothes help me stay healthy.

I put on my snowsuit, boots, hat, and mittens. Sometimes I put on a scarf.

Sometimes my mom or dad will help me put on my winter clothes.

Sometimes I walk outside into the cold air. I can look for a spot of snow close to the house away from the road to make my snow angel. I make sure that I am away from the trees and bushes so I will be safe.

Here's how I might make a snow angel:

1. I sit in the snow.

2. I can lay back so that I am looking straight up at the sky. I place my arms and legs straight out.

3. I move my arms through the snow, touching my hips, and then making my hands almost meet in the snow near my head.

4. I move my legs from side to side and then I stop.

5. I sit straight up.

6. I stand up and turn around to look at the angel I just made.

My snow angel is pretty. My snow angel stays outside.

Thunderstorms

Thunderstorms make a lot of noise.

The noise can be loud. I cannot see the thunder. I can hear it. I am safe inside.

Thunderstorms usually are short. When the storm is over, the thunder stops.

What to Do When it Rains

Rain comes and goes. If I want to know if it will rain today or tomorrow, I can listen to the weather report on the radio or on the television. The weather person makes a guess about the weather.

If I am outside when it begins to rain, I will try to go inside. If I stay outside, I will get wet.

If it starts to rain while I am at home or school, I will try to remember if I left any of my belongings outside. If something is outside, it will get wet in the rain.

If I did leave something outside, I will ask for permission to quickly go and get it. After I get it, I will bring it inside.

90

When the Lights Go Out

Sometimes when there is a thunderstorm, the lights may go out.

Sometimes when the lights go out, they might be off for a few seconds, a few minutes, or a few hours. To help myself, I can close my eyes or ask for a hug to comfort me.

Other people around me might need a hug, too. Hugging helps many people feel safe and secure.

Thunderstorms Are Okay

Flowers are pretty. Grass is green.

If the flowers and the grass didn't get water, they might die or look ugly. One way they get water is from rain that falls from the clouds.

Sometimes the weather makes a bright flash and a loud bang when it rains. This is lightning and thunder.

Sometimes the wind blows real strong, and I may hear the trees blowing outside.

If I look out the window, I may see the water falling on the flowers and the trees.

It's okay if there is lightning and thunder when it's raining.

I know the flowers and the grass will look pretty and make everybody happy.

Chapter 12

Holidays, Vacation

And Recreation

Valentine's Day

Valentine's Day is February 14.

On Valentine's Day I may show someone that I love them.

There are many things I can give to a person I care about. I can give candy, flowers, or a card.

I can make a card out of paper. I might draw big red hearts on the card.

I might make a valentine card for each person that I love.

Valentine's Day is a day to show people that I care about them.

The National Anthem

Sometimes the National Anthem is played or sung. It is a song that is special to our country.

Many people think that our country is special. They think that the National Anthem is special.

When the National Anthem is played, people stand up. There might even be a flag near me that I can look at while I listen to the song.

If I am wearing a hat, it's important to take it off until the National Anthem is done. This is a rule that helps us show respect for our country and flag.

The Fourth of July Fireworks

Every year I have a birthday. The country I live in has a birthday, too. It is on July 4.

For my birthday I have cake and open presents. When my country has a birthday, I sometimes celebrate with fireworks. I watch fireworks outside or on television.

Sometimes fireworks make loud noises and have bright lights.

BANG!

I will let an adult light the fireworks so that I will be safe.

The fireworks are safe. If I am frightened, I will hug my mom and dad. Hugging my mom or dad might help me feel safer.

When I Swim

When I swim on hot days, the water will cool me off. It is important to always swim with my family or friends. Swimming with other people helps to keep everyone safe.

Swimming is a form of exercise that makes people stronger.

When I swim, I will wear my life jacket so that I am safe. I will always have an adult watch me when I swim.

Vacations

Sometimes I have time off from school. This is called a vacation.

Vacations are a time when schools are closed. Once in a while, my family may take a vacation while school is open.

It is okay to be home on a weekday when I have a vacation.

Vacations are usually fun.

Sometimes vacations are one or two days.
Sometimes vacations are for one or two weeks.
Sometimes vacations are longer.

After the vacation, I can go back to school.

Going to the Zoo

Going to the zoo may be fun.

When I go to the zoo, I see many animals.

Animals are kept in cages or beyond barriers for my safety. Animals are kept in cages or beyond barriers for their safety, too.

The zoo is a great place to learn about animals.

Going to See a Play

Sometimes Mom and Dad will want to see a play.

A play is when people get dressed up in costumes and act out a story.

Sometimes a play will make me laugh. These plays are called comedies.

Sometimes a play will be serious. These plays are called dramas.

It's important to try to sit quietly during a play. If I need to talk, others will like it if I whisper softly. People around me are trying to hear the actors and actresses.

I will try to watch the play. I will try to listen to the play.

A Day Spent at the Ballpark

Sometimes Mom and Dad take me to a baseball game. The game could be a high school or major league game.

Sometimes the stadium is far away. It might take a long time to get there. I will try to be patient. I may play car games until we get there.

At the stadium, I get out of the car. I walk to the stadium with my mom and dad.

We find our seats. If I have to go to the toilet, I will tell Mom or Dad. They will take me to a toilet.

Sometimes I may get souvenirs. I can ask Mom or Dad to buy me a souvenir. Sometimes they say, "Yes." Sometimes they say, "No." Either way, I will try to be happy.

When I feel hungry, I can tell Mom or Dad. They might get me something to eat. They might ask me to wait.

The game usually lasts nine innings. If it starts to rain, the game might be postponed or canceled. This means the game may be continued at another time. Mom or Dad will know if they will be finishing the game. It is okay to leave a baseball stadium before the game is finished.

When the game is over, we get in the car and go home.

Sometimes we may stop to get something to eat.

Playing Video Games

Sometimes I play video games.

Sometimes I have many games to choose from. Not everyone has a lot of video games.

I might play by myself, or I might have someone play with me.

We will try to take turns playing the video game.

Sometimes I win the video game. Sometimes I lose the video game.

It is okay if I lose. I will try to be a *good sport*. A *good sport* is someone who plays fair. A *good sport* tries to stay calm when he or she loses.

Chapter 13

How to Write A

Social Story

How to Write a Social Story

What is a Social Story?

This author first defined Social Stories early in 1991. Since that time, experience with Social Stories and an increasing understanding of the approach has resulted in revisions of the original definition. Currently, a Social Story is considered as a *process* that results in a *product* for a person with an autistic spectrum disorder (ASD). First, as a process, a Social Story requires consideration of – and respect for – the perspective of the person with ASD. As a product, a Social Story is a short story – defined by specific characteristics - that describes a situation, concept, or social skill using a format that is meaningful for people with ASD. In this way, each Social Story addresses the needs and improves the social understanding of people on *both sides* of the social equation. The result is often renewed sensitivity of others to the experience of the person with ASD, and an improvement in the response of the person with ASD.

Who Writes Social Stories?

Social Stories are written by parents, teachers, neighbors, speech therapists, doctors, grandmas, occupational and physical therapists, uncles, psychologists, nephews, social workers, friends, dentists, aunts, grandpas, and siblings: people who work or live with people with ASD. For the purposes of this article, "author" refers to all of those who learn to write Social Stories.

Social Story Topics

Social Stories may be used to address a seemingly infinite number of topics. Social Stories are often written in response to a troubling situation, in an effort to provide a person with ASD with the social information he may be lacking. It often does not take long for a parent or professional to identify a situation where a Social Story may be helpful. For example, parents may notice their child has difficulty riding in the car, playing with other children, or expressing emotions. Sometimes, a person with ASD asks a question or makes a comment that indicates he is "misreading" a given situation, and a Social Story is developed.

In educational settings, Social Story topics are as varied and individual as the students for whom they are written. They may describe skills that are part of the academic or social curriculums, personalize social skills covered in a social skills training program, or translate a goal into understandable steps. Often, Social Stories are used to describe a classroom routine, including variations in that routine. For example, a Social Story may describe the factors that may lead to the cancellation of outdoor recess, or the use of substitute teachers. In addition, every school experience includes field trips, fire and tornado drills, carnivals, open houses, and assemblies. A teacher may write a Social Story to describe each special event in advance.

Social Stories have another purpose that is equally important and frequently overlooked: acknowledging achievement. In fact, a child's first Social Story should describe a skill or situation that is *typically successful and problem-free*. This makes it easier for a child to identify with a story from start to finish before tackling more challenging topics. Plus, written praise may be far more meaningful for children with ASD than its verbal counterpart. For these reasons, at least half of the Social Stories developed for a child with ASD should bring attention to positive achievements. This creates a permanent record of what a child does well: information that is important in building a positive self-esteem.

A Social Story has defining characteristics that distinguish it from a traditional task analysis, social script, or other visual strategy. The most important elements of a Social Story are four basic sentence types and a ratio that defines their frequency. In addition, *how* each sentence is written is equally important. The next two sections describe the types of Social Story sentences and their ratio, and discuss *The Social Story Guidelines* that ensure the patient and reassuring quality that is characteristic of every Social Story.

The Basic Social Story Sentences and Ratio

There are four basic sentence types: *descriptive, perspective, affirmative,* and *directive.* Each has a specific role. Each sentence type is used in a Social Story according to a specified frequency, called the *Social Story Ratio.* Understanding the types of sentences in a Social Story, and their role and relationship to the overall impact of a story, is the first step to writing effective Social Stories.

<u>Descriptive sentences</u> are truthful, opinion-and-assumption-free statements of fact. They identify the most relevant factors in a situation or the most important aspects of the topic. *The only required type of sentence in a Social Story and the most frequently used,* descriptive sentences form the "backbone" of a Social Story. They often contain the answers to the important "wh" questions that guide story development. The objectivity of descriptive sentences brings *logic and accuracy* to a Social Story – two qualities likely to be reassuring to those who are overwhelmed by social concepts and situations. Sample descriptive sentences include:

1) My name is _____ (often the first sentence in a Social Story).
2) Sometimes, my grandmother reads to me.
3) Many children play on the playground during outdoor recess.

<u>Perspective sentences</u> are statements that refer to, or describe, a person's internal state, their knowledge/thoughts, feelings, beliefs, opinions, motivation, or physical condition/health. Only on rare occasions are perspective sentences used that describe or refer to the internal status of the person with ASD; most frequently they are used to refer to the internal status of *other* people. These sentences give a Social Story a "heart", describing the emotional and cognitive aspects that are a (sometimes invisible but critically important) part of every social situation. Sample perspective sentences include:

1) My teacher or substitute knows about math (knowledge/thoughts).
2) My sister usually likes to play the piano (feelings).
3) Some children believe in the Easter Bunny (belief).
4) Many children like peanut butter and jelly sandwiches for lunch (opinion).
5) Some children decide to work hard to finish assignments before recess (motivation).
6) Sometimes, people feel sick when they eat too much (physical condition/health).

Directive sentences identify a suggested response or choice of responses to a situation or concept, gently directing the behavior of the person with ASD. Authors must carefully develop these sentences, paying special attention to the possibility of literal interpretation. For example, beginning a directive sentence with *I will* or *I can* may mislead a person with ASD, who may believe the response must be completed exactly as written, with no room for error. Instead, directive sentences often begin with *I will try to...*, *I will work on...*, or *One thing I may try to say (do) is...* . Directive sentences may also be stated as a series of response options. Sample directive sentences include:
1) I will try to stay in my chair.
2) I may ask Mom or Dad for a hug.
3) On the playground, I may decide to play on the swings, on the monkey bars, or maybe with something else.

Affirmative sentences (named by Jo Bromley, England) enhance the meaning of surrounding statements, often expressing a commonly shared value or opinion within a given culture. (Statements representing an opinion that is *specific* to an individual or smaller group are *not* affirmative sentences.) Specifically, the role of an affirmative statement is to stress an important point, refer to a law or rule, or reassure the person with ASD. Usually, affirmative sentences immediately follow a descriptive, perspective, or directive sentence. Sample affirmative sentences include (in italics):
1) Most people eat dinner before dessert. *This is a good idea* (stressing an important point).
2) I will try to keep my seat belt fastened. *This is very important* (reference to a law).
3) One child slides down the water slide at a time. *This is a safe thing to do* (reference to a rule).
4) The toilet makes a sound when it flushes. *This is okay* (reassure).

Partial sentences encourage a person with ASD to make guesses regarding the next step in a situation, the response of another individual, or his own response. They are very similar to fill-in-the-blank sentences that are often used by teachers in examinations to check understanding. In a Social Story, a descriptive, perspective, directive, or affirmative sentence may be written as a partial statement, with a portion of the sentence replaced with a blank space. In the process of reviewing a Social Story, the author encourages the person with ASD to complete the unfinished statement. For example, following a series of sentences describing why children have to sometimes stand and walk in lines at school, a partial perspective sentence may conclude the story with, *My teacher will probably feel_____ if I stand and walk in a line quietly.* By completing the sentence and filling in the blank, the student with ASD has to retrieve critical information. This may be an important step in demonstrating comprehension and independently applying the information to standing and walking in lines at school.

The Basic Social Story Ratio defines the relationship between the different types of Social Story sentences. Specifically, a Social Story has a ratio of two to five descriptive, perspective and/or affirmative sentences for every directive sentence. In some cases, directive sentences may not be necessary. The ratio applies when the story is considered as a whole. For example, a story could begin with seven descriptive sentences and close with two directive sentences, and still adhere to the *Basic Social Story Ratio*. This ratio ensures the descriptive quality of every Social Story:

0 - 1 (partial or complete) directive sentences   = Basic Social Story Ratio

2 - 5 (partial or complete) descriptive, perspective, and/or affirmative sentences

Additional Sentence Types and the Complete Social Story Ratio

There are two additional types of sentences that may also be used in a Social Story: *control sentences* and *cooperative sentences.* Although they are not used as frequently as the basic sentences, they represent important ideas that may also be included in a Social Story. Specifically, they represent the role of the person with ASD in determining his own new responses, and the efforts of others in the ultimate success of the person with ASD.

Control sentences are statements that are written by a person with ASD to identify personal strategies to use to recall and apply information. A control sentence often reflects individual interests or a favorite writing style. First, the person with ASD reviews the Social Story, adding one or more control sentences. For example, Benjamin, nine-years-old and an expert on insects, becomes upset whenever someone says, "I changed my mind!" After reading a Social Story about what people actually *mean* when they say that, Benjamin develops this sentence: *When someone says, "I changed my mind", I can think of an idea becoming better – like a caterpillar, changing into a butterfly.*

Cooperative sentences identify what others will do to assist the student (developed by Dr. Demetrious Haracopos, Denmark). For example, in a toileting story, a cooperative sentence may read: *My mom, dad, and teachers will help me as I learn to use the toilet.* In this way, cooperative sentences remind parents, peers, and/or professionals of their role in the success of the person with ASD. They may also describe a consistent response. A cooperative sentence may be written as a partial statement to help a person with ASD identify others who may assist him as he learns a new skill, and *how* they can help. For example, *People who can help me get my boots on are_____,* or *When I feel frustrated, others can help me by_____.*

Combinations of sentence types are possible. For example, the sentence, *My mom and dad will try to remain calm while I learn to use the toilet,* could be identified as either a perspective or cooperative sentence. One word of caution: If a sentence appears to meet the criteria for sentence types that are on *opposite* sides of the Social Story Ratio, the sentence probably needs to be re-written to clarify its meaning.

The Complete Social Story Ratio is similar to the Basic Social Story Ratio. It includes the basic Social Story sentences (descriptive, perspective, affirmative, and directive) *and* control and cooperative sentences. Like the Basic Social Story Ratio, the *Complete Social Story Ratio* ensures that the text focuses on *describing* an event, concept, or skill:

0 - 1 (partial or complete) directive or control sentences = Complete Social Story Ratio

2 - 5 (partial or complete) descriptive, perspective,
affirmative, or cooperative sentences

The Social Story Guidelines

As mentioned earlier, the *Social Story Guidelines* define a Social Story. They are based on the learning characteristics of people with ASD. Organized into four basic steps, they ensure that every Social Story has a patient and reassuring quality. The Social Story Guidelines set the standard for writing a Social Story without limiting creativity. There is plenty of room for inventive tailoring to meet the needs of the intended reader, or to incorporate new ideas.

Step 1. Picture the goal: The general goal of a Social Story is to *share accurate social information,* to *describe more than direct*. Picturing the goal requires an author to translate social information into meaningful text and illustrations. In many cases, this means describing abstract concepts and ideas with visual, concrete references and images. Therefore, while the end result of a Social Story may be a change in the response of the person with ASD, the *first priority* – the *goal* - is always to *share relevant social information* in a *meaningful way.*

Step 2. Gather information: Once a clear picture of the goal is established, the author gathers information about the topic. This includes *where* and *when* the situation occurs, *who* is involved, *how* events are sequenced, *what* occurs, and *why*. In addition, information about the learning style, reading ability, attention span, and interests of the person with ASD is collected. This information is gathered by interviewing those involved with the person with ASD: parents, professionals, and if possible, the person with ASD.

Observation of the person with ASD and the situation also provides important information. If possible, an author observes a situation first-hand. At the same time, consideration is given to possible variations in the routine or extraneous variables. For example, a gym class is scheduled for Tuesdays at 10:30. Sometimes, gym may be cancelled or rescheduled to allow for a special activity. By recognizing factors that may alter a situation and writing those variations into a Social Story, each story prepares a person with ASD for the possibility of unexpected changes. Therefore, the sentence, *Gym is usually Tuesdays at 10:30*, is far more accurate than the sentence; *Gym is Tuesdays at 10:30*. The latter sentence, if interpreted literally, may be inaccurate much of the time, as the exact time for gym may vary, and other activities may occasionally be substituted in its place.

13-5

Observing the person with ASD in the target situation yields insight into what may be motivating his current response. An author observes the situation from the perspective of the person with ASD and asks himself, "What would cause *me* to respond that way?" It's important for the author to recognize his own limitations in accurately assuming the perspective of a person with ASD. He must keep in mind: responses that to him seem "out of the blue" or inappropriate may be entirely logical when considered from the perspective of the person with ASD. In this way, the author makes a serious attempt to view the social environment from the perspective of the person with ASD in an effort to identify information that person may be missing or misinterpreting. This information determines the *focus* of a Social Story, in other words, what to include in a story and what can be omitted.

Step 3. Tailor the text: The author customizes the text to the learning style, needs, interests, and abilities of the person with ASD. This results in a *Social Story*, a story with the following defining characteristics:

1) A Social Story has an introduction, body, and conclusion.

2) A Social Story answers "wh" questions, including *who* is involved, *where* and *when* a situation occurs, *what* is happening, *how* it happens, and *why*.

3) A Social Story is written from a first person perspective, i.e. as though the person with ASD is describing the event or concept, and occasionally from a third person perspective, like a newspaper article (advanced).

4) A Social Story is written in positive language, with positively stated descriptions of responses and behaviors. If a reference to a negative behavior is made, it is done with caution and from a third person – rather than specific first or second person – perspective. For example, *Sometimes people may unintentionally say something to hurt another person's feelings. This is a mistake.*

5) A Social Story contains up to four basic types of Social Story sentences (descriptive, perspective, affirmative, and directive) that occur in a proportion specified by the Basic Social Story Ratio (0-1 partial or complete directive sentences for every 2-5 partial or complete descriptive, perspective, and/or affirmative sentences). Possibly up to six sentence types (with the addition of control and/or cooperative sentences) that occur in a proportion specified by the Complete Social Story Ratio (0-1 partial or complete directive and/or control sentences for every 2-5 partial or complete descriptive, perspective, affirmative, and/or cooperative sentences).

6) A Social Story is *literally accurate* (can be interpreted literally without altering intended meaning of text and illustrations), with use of "insurance policy" words like *usually* and *sometimes* to ensure that accuracy.

7) A Social Story may use alternative vocabulary to maintain its relaxed and positive quality. (For example, the first word in each of the following pairs may elicit anxiety, it is followed by a possible alternative word in italics: different = *another*, change = *replace*, new = *better*.)

8) A Social Story uses concrete, easy to understand text enhanced by visual supports if needed (translating abstract concepts into tangible, visually based terminology and illustration).

9) A Social Story may contain illustrations to clarify and enhance the meaning of the text. Illustrations are frequently helpful in stories for young children, or for those who are more severely challenged. If illustrations are used, they reflect consideration of the age and personal learning characteristics of the person with ASD.

10) A style and format that is motivating, or reflects the interests of, the person with ASD.

Step 4. Teach with the title: The title of a Social Story states the overall meaning or "gist" of the Social Story, following the applicable characteristics listed in Step 3. References to any behaviors – positive or negative - are rarely a part of a Social Story title. Sometimes, a title may be stated as a question, with the story answering the question. Whether as a statement or question, the title identifies and reinforces the most important information in the Social Story.

Putting It All Together: Is this a Social Story? Writing a Social Story, especially the first few times, can be a little, well... scary. For that reason, people who attend Social Story workshops write their first story as part of a team to generate ideas, catch errors, and provide immediate feedback. For those writing Social Stories on their own, it's still possible to critically review a story. *The Social Story Checklist* (Appendix A) may be used to compare a Social Story with its defining characteristics. In addition, an author may ask others for constructive feedback and suggestions. For example, members of a student's educational team may routinely share drafts of a Social Story. Whether an author is writing his first or fiftieth story, using a team to *review* and *revise* the text and illustrations results in a story that adheres to the guidelines. Working with a team also results in a Social Story that is comfortable for all those involved in its implementation. It's interesting to note that a Social Story is at its best when authors *are social:* demonstrating cooperation, problem solving, and effective social skills while completing the text, illustrations, and plans for implementation.

Guidelines for Implementing a Social Story

Taking care when sharing a Social Story with a person with ASD is an important factor in its effectiveness. The guidelines for introducing and implementing a Social Story have their roots in the common sense and expertise of authors; relying on the knowledge and "intuition" of those who know the person with ASD best. Listed here are suggestions to guide the important decisions surrounding the use of a Social Story, sketching an outline to be completed with individualized details.

Introducing a Social Story The manner in which a Social Story is introduced is consistent with its patient and reassuring quality. Following review of a draft of a Social Story by important individuals, it is introduced to the person with ASD in a relaxed setting. This is important, as anxiety can undermine positive learning, and in the long term may adversely impact how the person with ASD regards Social Stories. Sharing a Social Story while a difficult or upsetting event is occurring, or when a person with ASD is upset, is avoided. In addition, using review of a Social Story as a punitive consequence for misbehavior is inappropriate.

Honesty is the most important element when a Social Story is initially introduced. A simple, straightforward phrase is all that is needed to start things off. For example, the author may begin with, "I wrote this story for you", or "I have a story about Snack Time. It's time for us to read it together". Once accustomed to Social Stories, a person with ASD may initiate a request for a story on a specific topic. In this case, the opening for introducing the story may be, "You asked me to write a Social Story for you about lunch time. I finished it. Would you like to read it?" Caution is used when phrasing the introduction of a Social Story to a person with ASD. In the previous example, if the last question is interpreted literally it is an invitation to the person with ASD to accept, or reject, reading the story. If this choice is not intended, it is preferable to say, "Soon, it's time to look at this story together."

Reviewing a Social Story A Social Story is reviewed with a prevailing positive, casual, and comfortable attitude. This is perhaps the most important element in the implementation of a Social Story. Every other aspect of an implementation plan is likely to fail without a patient and positive backdrop.

Remember Jiminy Cricket? His teaching style is applicable to the implementation of a Social Story with a young child. The author sits to the child's side and slightly back, or positions the child comfortably on his lap. *Attention is jointly focused on the Social Story* and away from the face or gestures of the author. This is the "Jiminy Cricket" position, named after the friend of Pinocchio in the classic children's story, who, though often out of Pinocchio's direct visual field, would gently guide his actions with advice. The author reads the Social Story with a friendly, gentle tone that matches the patient and reassuring quality of the text.

Once a story has been introduced and read with a person with ASD, asking others to review the story with the person with ASD is often helpful. People are selected who are important in the story, or directly impacted by the story's content. The story is then shared with those individuals one-at-a-time, encouraging each of them to read the story aloud. The reasons for this are threefold: 1) others physically demonstrate to the person with ASD that they now have the same information; 2) it allows for immediate review of the story within the social context of sharing it with others; and 3) it encourages generalization of the story to other settings and situations. For example, a Social Story describing the need for an occasional substitute (supply) teacher is first reviewed by a consultant and Jose, a nine-year-old student. Then, the story is shared with Jose's teachers, speech therapist, and physical therapist. This involvement of others soon after a story is introduced fosters cooperation and consistency.

Common sense underwrites every Social Story, and similarly guides when, and how, it is reviewed. Stories are typically introduced one at a time, allowing time to focus on one concept or skill, and avoiding the possibility of being overwhelmed with too much information. Many Social Stories are initially reviewed once a day, others just prior to the situation they describe. The topic of a Social Story also will impact on the review schedule that is used. For example, stories about the holiday season may be reviewed within a few weeks to a few days of the event. In contrast, a Social Story describing a social skill that is used in a variety of settings may be reviewed each day, perhaps with the addition of new details as comprehension and application of the information increases. The most important aspect of a review schedule is an individual knowledge of the person with ASD and the situation, along with healthy common sense.

Fading a Social Story   There are a few strategies that may gradually increase the independence of a person with ASD and his command of the information in a Social Story. However, experience indicates it may not be possible, or advisable, to fade a Social Story from use. This section shares a few ideas as to how – and when – to fade a Social Story.

One of the simplest ways to fade a Social Story is to re-write it. In this case, selected sentences are either omitted or revised. For example, once a child seems confident with a new skill or concept, the directive sentences in the Social Story may be omitted. Or, instead of eliminating these sentences completely, they may be re-written as partial sentences. This encourages a child to recall the information with the support of the author. A word of caution: omitting and revising sentences *changes* the story format. This may be upsetting for some people with ASD. If this is the case, consider an alternative to making changes in the text or illustrations of the story.

Another strategy for increasing independence does not require any revision of the original story. Instead, the review schedule for the story is "expanded", leaving a gradually increasing amount of time between review sessions. For example, instead of reading a story daily, the story may be reviewed four times a week. Occasionally, a person with ASD will provide feedback on his need to review a story, refusing to "read it now" or indicating, "I know all that stuff". In this case, it is advisable to place the story in an accessible location, while moving on to another activity.

Sometimes, Social Stories may *consistently* elicit a defensive posture from an individual. There may be several reasons for this. Sometimes, a person may become understandably defensive when attention is repeatedly focused on areas of difficulty. (This may be prevented by frequently presenting Social Stories that praise achievements and strengths.) Other factors may also result in refusal to review a story. Care should be taken to understand and respond accordingly so that Social Stories do not become an activity that elicits negative emotions or responses. A person with ASD has many challenges; whenever an intended solution begins to look more like a new problem, it requires everyone to re-think the process and its goals.

Summary

In summary, a Social Story is a product and a process that improves social understanding between people with ASD and those who work on their behalf. As a process, authors consider information and events through the eyes of the person with

ASD. As a product, a Social Story is defined by specific characteristics that translate social information into text, illustrations, and titles that are meaningful for people with autistic spectrum disorders. The result is often an improvement in social understanding on both sides of the social equation. Equipped with paper, pencils, computers, and a renewed social understanding of one another, it is hoped Social Stories will continue to be an important vehicle that brings people with ASD and those working on their behalf closer to one another.

Appendix A: The Social Story Checklist

Directions: This checklist compares a story with the defining characteristics of a Social Story. The comparison helps to identify strengths and areas that may need revision.

*Title of story*_____ *Author*_____

*The story is written for*_____

Carefully read the story aloud and place a check (tick) in the appropriate blank:

	YES	NO
1. Is there an introduction, body, and conclusion?	___	___
2. Does the story answer the relevant "wh" questions? Sometimes, many of these questions may be answered in a single (often opening) statement.	___	___
3. If the story is written for a young student, is it written from a first person perspective, as though the student is describing the event? Or, if the story is for an older student or adult, is it written from a third person perspective, similar to a newspaper article?	___	___
4. Does the story have a positive tone? If negative information is included, is it stated carefully using a third person perspective?	___	___
5. Does the story adhere to either Social Story Ratio (Basic or Complete)? (0-1 partial or complete directive and/or control sentences for every 2-5 partial or complete descriptive, perspective, affirmative, or cooperative sentences = The Complete Social Story Ratio)	___	___
6. Is the story literally accurate? Can it be interpreted literally without altering the intended meaning?	___	___
7. Is alternative vocabulary used in place of terms that may cause the person with ASD to become upset or nervous?	___	___
8. Is the text written with consideration of reading ability and attention span of the person with ASD, using visual supports to enhance the meaning of the story?	___	___
9. If illustrations are used, are they developed and presented with consideration of the ability of the person with ASD?	___	___
10. Has an effort been made to incorporate the student's interests into the format, content, illustrations, or implementation of the story?	___	___
11. *Overall*, does the story have a patient and reassuring quality?	___	___